BOOK ANALYSIS

Written by Vincent Jooris
Translated by Emma Lunt

AF131424

The Red and the Black

BY STENDHAL

STENDHAL

FRENCH WRITER AND ART CRITIC

- **Born in 1783 in Grenoble**
- **Died in 1842 in Paris**
- **Notable work:**
  - *Vanina Vanina* (1829), short story
  - *The Red and the Black* (1830), novel
  - *The Charterhouse of Parma* (1839), novel

Stendhal, whose real name was Henri Beyle, was born in Grenoble in 1783 to a bourgeois family. In Paris, under the Directory, he was impassioned by the debates which sharpened his critical spirit. He discovered Italy and Germany during military campaigns as part of Bonaparte's army. After 1815, he became an art critic in Milan and wrote touristic works which he signed under his pseudonym. From 1830, Louis-Philippe named him French Consul in Trieste and then Civitavecchia. It was here that he completed his most famous novels (*The Red and the Black* (1830), *The Charterhouse of Parma* (1839)) and an autobiography (*The Life of Henry Brulard* (1835-1836)). A stroke brought him back to Paris in 1841. He died the following year, leaving several manuscripts incomplete.

THE RED AND THE BLACK

THE REMARKABLE DESTINY OF JULIEN SOREL

- **Genre:** novel
- **Reference edition:** Stendhal (2004) *The Red and the Black*. Trans. Raffel, B. New York: Modern Library Classics.
- **First edition:** 1830
- **Themes:** love, ambition, initiation, disillusion, adultery, youth, social classes

The Red and the Black was published in November 1830, but did not gain the same level of success at the time that it has today.

The story takes place between 1826 and 1830 and mainly tells the story of the romantic relationship between Julien Sorel, a young seminarian and Madame de Rênal, an older lady whose husband doesn't understand her.

The title of the book has been subject to many different interpretations. For some people it symbolises military uniform (which Julien dreamt of wearing) and a priest's cassock (Julien eventually dedicates himself to an ecclesiastical career). Others see the black as hypocrisy, while Julien prefers the red of sacrifice. Others still link the title to the colours used in games of chance (such as roulette or cards) or political parties.

SUMMARY

PART ONE

Chapters 1-7

Verrières is a small, imaginary village in the Franche-Comté. Julien Sorel is the third-born son of a carpenter. As the child's thirst for education causes his father's contempt, Father Chélan takes him under his wing: Julien recites the New Testament with him, all the while being secretly fascinated by Napoléon Bonaparte's life.

At the priest's recommendation, Monsieur de Rênal hires Sorel to tutor his children. The young, shy man therefore finds his way into the province's world of bourgeoisie. Madame de Rênal shows an innocent interest in him.

Chapters 8-17

When Elisa, the de Rênals' maid, receives an inheritance, she sets her sights on marrying Julien, but he refuses. Relieved, Madame de Rênal is surprised by her feelings towards the tutor.

At the Vergy family castle, Julien begins to seduce Madame de Rênal. He progresses slowly until, despite his clumsiness, he successfully gets into her bedroom. Madame de Rênal swings between feeling guilty and showing her affection. As for Julien, his calculated coldness finally gives way to true feelings.

Chapters 18-23

An unnamed king arrives in Verrières. Thanks to Madame de Rênal, Julien acts as a ceremonial guard for the occasion, which raises suspicions. Sorel watches the Bishop of Agde's ceremonial procession which revives his ecclesiastical ambition.

The de Rênals' youngest son falls ill, which reawakens his mother's guilt. Rumours of her relationship fly and Monsieur de Rênal receives an anonymous letter warning him. Using a fake letter, the woman manages to provisionally quell her husband's doubts.

Julien dines at the Valenods' house. The Valenod family have a rivalry with the de Rênals over control of Verrières.

Warned of Julien's adultery by Elisa, Father Chélan demands that he leave Verrières for the seminary in Besançon. Julien agrees to go, but promises Madame de Rênal that he will come back to see her regularly.

Chapters 24-28

At an inn in Besançon, Julien meets Amanda Binet. At the seminary, Father Pirard tests Julien with a long interview during which Sorel faints. The young man becomes his envious classmates' target. Father Frilair catches him out in the exams.

Chapters 29-30

At the advice of Father Pirard, the Marquis de La Mole hires

Julien as his secretary. One night, the young man returns to Verrières to see Madame de Rênal once again. She hides him, but the following night he has to flee, chased by Monsieur de Rênal's gunshots.

PART TWO

Chapters 1-6

Julien goes to the Marquis de la Mole's house in Paris. The marquis' daughter, Mathilde, irritates Sorel greatly. A misunderstanding leads to Julien challenging a knight to a duel and, in order to protect his honour, the knight leads Julien to believe he is the marquis' biological son.

Chapters 7-20

Monsieur Valenod becomes the new mayor of Verrières. The Marquis de la Mole, who is already very courteous, becomes even friendlier with Julien. Mathilde, engaged to the Marquis de Croisenois (one of her many suitors), imagines the boring life that lies ahead of her.

A ball takes place in the Retz hotel. Mathilde is attracted by Julien's political statements, appreciating his originality. The two young adults have many debates. Julien gives her an insight into his revolutionary beliefs. Mathilde then falls in love with the young man but he doesn't trust her. Mathilde writes to him to arrange to meet up. He is hesitant, but goes and she wins him over. It seems to be more of a planned love than a passionate love. The couple alternate between arguing and reconciling, between happiness and disappointment.

Chapters 21-28

The Marquis de la Mole tasks Julien with a mission; to be a secretary during a meeting of aristocratic royalist conspirators and then send a report to Strasbourg. When he arrives in Strasbourg, he listens to Prince Korasoff's romantic advice. On returning to Paris, Sorel woos and talks with his chosen "prey": the the Marechale of Fervaques. He rewrites the love letters that Korasoff had given him as examples. During a dinner at the Marechale de Fervaques house, Julien bumps into Mathilde who he had almost forgotten about. Seeing him courting the Marechale, Mathilde falls in love with him once again.

Chapters 29-34

Mathilde meets up with Julien. When she finds out about his little letter-writing game with the Marechale de Fervaques, she is annoyed and then regretful for having made Julien suffer at the hands of her pride. Sorel puts on a cold front, then wins Mathilde over again.

Mathilde tells her father that she is pregnant; the marquis is furious and Julien flees. Eventually, the Marquis de la Mole decides to take things into his own hands; he ennobles Sorel and grants him the position of lieutenant of hussars. The young man celebrates, but the marquis still avoids bring up the issue of marriage.

Chapter 35

Madame de Rênal's confessor encourages her to send a letter to the marquis, in which she denounces Julien's immoral desires. Any possibility of marriage between him and Mathilde is therefore cancelled. In a fit of rage, Sorel rushes to Verrières. In the middle of mass, he shoots Madame de Rênal twice and is arrested.

Chapters 36-45

While imprisoned in Besançon, he learns that Madame de Rênal has survived. Paradoxically, Julien loves her even more when he hears this and regrets having attempted to kill her.

He also reflects on the future of Mathilde and his child; he tells her to marry Croisenois. Mathilde tries to save him through various means; most significantly, she goes to Father Frilair, who assures her that he can influence the jury and the public prosecutors; in return he wants to be bishop. Father Chélan and Fouqué visit Julien but he refuses to see his father. Madame de Rênal also writes to the jury, asking for them to be lenient.

Julien is no longer ambitious. He neglects his defence and his plea is just an accusation of the bourgeois class. The court condemns him to death.

Mathilde wants him to appeal but he refuses; when Madame de Rênal asks him to, he agrees. Mathilde is depressed. Sorel finally agrees to see his father. Julien refuses to let Madame de Rênal request the king's pardon. He faces death resolutely and is executed.

Mathilde buries Julien's head. Madame de Rênal dies three days later.

CHARACTER STUDY

JULIEN SOREL

At the start of the novel, Julien is 19 years old and at the end, in 1830, he is 23. He is motherless, has a father that despises him and is his brothers' scapegoat. He is a young man who is eager to learn, living with a family who don't understand him and whom he hates. He is distrustful, and sees mockery and teasing everywhere: 'he was a miserable man at war with all of society' (Part 2, Chapter 13).

His physical appearance gives an impression of youthful fragility, despite the sobriety of his gaze: 'to her deep pleasure, she'd seen the shy demeanour of a young girl in this fateful tutor, though on her children's account she'd dreaded his harsh surliness' (Part 1, Chapter 6).

In this hostile world, Julien responds with hypocrisy. But, despite the mask he wears, he cannot constantly hide his true personality. This makes those he speaks to feel somewhat uncomfortable, as they can explicitly see his disdain for vulgarity and his ambition: 'I see something in you which offends coarse soul. Jealousy and slander will hound you. Where Providence may place you, your colleagues will never see you without hating you' (Part 1, Chapter 29).

The narrator often uses the expression 'our hero' to describe him, and intervenes to argue his case or to simply give his opinion. The narrator gives his private thoughts here and there, such as "what pity for our country bumpkin" (Part 1,

Chapter 24).

Furthermore, the narrator maintains the collusion between the reader and Sorel by revealing the latter's internal thoughts. These monologues are particularly suited to a solitary hero who hides everything, both his intentions and his vulnerability. Through this same process, the narrator also notices Madame de Rênal's growing love, before she was even aware of it herself, and transcribes Mathilde's passionate turnarounds.

MADAME DE RÊNAL

Her religious education and her marriage at the age of 16 have caused her to miss out on a lot of life experience. Emotional, naïve and secretive, she doesn't realise that she is bored of her husband. Therefore, the education of her three children is her main priority.

> "She was a tall, well-made woman, who had been the local beauty, as people in these mountains put it. There was a distinct straightforwardness about her, and in the youthful spring of her walk: indeed, to the eyes of a Parisian such unspoiled charm, as innocent as it was lively, might even have seemed suggestive of a sweet sensuality...She had never in her life been tempted either to flirtation or any manner of affected behaviour" (Part, 1, Chapter 3).

In part two, Julien often argues with Mathilde. Madame de Rênal plays the woman who consoles and forgives him.

MATHILDE

While the first part of the novel focuses on the relationship between Julien and Madame de Rênal, Mathilde de la Mole intervenes in part two. She is arrogant, and looks sarcastically on the behaviour of those that displease her. While considering her suitors, we see that: 'she did not think such people had been fashioned to understand her; had it been a question of buying a carriage, or a piece of property, she would have consulted them' (Part 2, Chapter 14).

An energetic and demanding character, she admires heroism and action, which is what causes her to fall in love with Julien. Sorel isn't interested in her at first due to her hypocrisy and arrogance.

> "Julien believed Mademoiselle de La Mole possessed of the conniving nature of Machiavelli. A pose of such wickedness was, in her eyes, quite charming-almost the only moral charm she enjoyed. Boredom, generated by hypocrisy and all his virtuous talk, threw him into such immoderate judgments. It was his imagination he was exciting, rather than letting himself be swept up by love" (Part 2, Chapter 12).
> "I've learned how to love this prideful monster" (Part 2, Chapter 35).

She turns out to be the female double of Julien. They see one another as equals or as rivals, which explains their movement between attraction and repulsion and their contradictory behaviour. On the other hand, when he is imprisoned, Mathilde's attitude prompts Julien's scorn.

SECONDARY CHARACTERS

- Julien's father, a violent and miserly carpenter;
- Monsieur de Rênal, the vain Mayor of Verrières ;
- The Rênal children, the only human beings to whom Julien will show his sensitivity;
- The Marquis de La Mole. Although Julien thought he was disrespectful, he shows himself to be more protective and friendly than Monsieur de Rênal;
- The supplementary characters: Elisa, Amanda Binet, Fouqué and Madame Derville. They give psychological depth to the two main protagonists;
- The politicians of Verrières: Moirod, Cholin and above all, the de Rênals' rivals, the Valenods;
- The aristocrats;
- The members of the clergy.

ANALYSIS

SUBJECTIVE REALISM

Realism is a literary and artistic trend which began halfway through the 19th century. Realist writers tried to describe reality as best they could. Balzac, a prominent realist author, depicted the social environment in which his characters evolved as scrupulously and objectively as possible.

Although he was writing at the start of the century, Stendhal took a realist approach and painted a precise picture of the social context. He also drew inspiration for his plot from legal cases that were taking place at the time, which is also a realist method. Both the case of Antoine Berthet (*La Gazette des tribunaux*, December 1827) and of Adrien Lafargue (1829), who both murdered their mistresses, served as initial material for his story.

However, he differentiates himself from realists in the fact that in his stories, reality is only seen through the protagonists' eyes. Indeed, in *The Red and the Black*, the reader only sees the world through Julien's eyes and they only know what he retains.

Furthermore, like Montesquieu (in *Persian Letters*) and Voltaire (in *The Huron*), Stendhal throws his hero into a society where he feels like an outsider: the naïve view through which Julien views the establishments in turn becomes a satire of society. Therefore, Stendhal adopts a critical realism approach.

In fact, this 'Chronicle of the 19th century' (the novel's sub-title) represents Restoration society in which people clashed and reigned supreme:

- The bourgeoisie (symbolised by the Verrières), rich and reactionary.
- The clergy (Besançon), whose meddling knows no bounds.
- The aristocracy (Paris), full of its own privileges.

Yet the new generation, who had grown up during the Napoleonic wars and seen the Bourbons' return, also wanted glory, ambition and power. But the prospect of rapid ascension didn't exist in this gerontocratic society that refused new ideas. Therefore, Julien represents the experience of most French youths at this time. 'Truth, bitter truth' is a quote by Danton which is used as the epigraph for the first part of the novel and summarises what Stendhal is writing. He wants to show the reality of the era, when young people had to choose between the army and religion and could follow no other path.

JULIEN'S AMBITION

Julien Sorel wants to escape his current status and dreams of climbing the social ladder. He has no connections and therefore only has his intelligence to help him. But Sorel turns to two people to inspire his acts:

- Napoleon. Julien read the *Mémorial de Sainte-Hélène* by Las Cases and kept a portrait of the emperor. For him, Napoleon is a model of success: he was a relatively poor young man but he was audacious and climbed his way up through society of his own accord. Stendhal, like his hero, Julien Sorel, was a Bonapartist; he also refers to Napoleon in *The Charterhouse of Parma*.

- Tartuffe. Molière's character is a pretend devotee; his fake humility hides his fierce ambition.

To climb his way up, the young man adopts a plan based on hypocrisy: he never reveals his true feelings and certainly not his intentions, and the things he does don't correspond with his thoughts. He views the world through cynical eyes. In a way, this works as a legitimate defence.

Furthermore, an ecclesiastical career seems to him to be a good way to work his way up the social hierarchy. In becoming a tutor for the de Rênals, he gets his foot in the door of the provincial bourgeoisie. Then, while working for the marquis, he infiltrates the aristocracy. But, secretly, he can't help but curse his new entourage, who represent the high society from which he is excluded. As he leaves from dinner at the Valenods, after small talk and dry conversation, he curses 'Ah, scum! Scum!' (Part 1, Chapter 22).

In his ambitious plan, female conquests are also important. Julien views seduction like a military battle, using the same terminology to describe the two. At the start, he leaves no room for feelings. After spending the night with a lover, the only pleasure he feels comes from having accomplished his mission. Having qualms would risk dulling his passion and distracting him from his goal, so he refuses to show any feelings. Furthermore, it is Julien who creates these rules for himself, but clarifies that while he feels the need to create these rules, it is because he is not naturally a hypocrite.

JULIEN'S MISTAKES

While, in theory, Julien's objective seems well planned, the reality proves to be very different from what he had expected. In fact, he starts something that he cannot stop, and the incidents follow one after the other, mistake after mistake.

- Naivety: throughout the story, Julien turns out to be more naïve than he wanted to be. To his astonishment, the young, shy man discovers the ugly happenings hidden and glossed over by the social groups who he becomes involved with. He innocently uses the letter of advice given to him by Prince Korassoff on the art of seduction.
- Misunderstandings. There are many mix-ups in the story (such as the duel). These mishaps are often embarrassing for Julien, and draw him away from his initial logic.
- Sympathy. When he arrives at the marquis' house, Julien expects to see yet more arrogance and pretentiousness like in Monsieur de Rênal's house. He thinks he is dealing with the enemy class. However, the Marquis de la Mole's consideration causes a crack in Julien's certainties, which threatens his resolution.
- Emotions. Julien is no Don Juan and, wanting to play the seducer, is caught in his own trap. The pride of possessing something and being admired doesn't really satisfy him, particularly with Madame de Rênal. He cannot stop himself wanting to feel the joy of tenderness. At the end of his existence, he discovers the true meaning of life.

- Sincerity. Julien is not naturally good at hiding things. He is sensitive and (therefore) easily offended, clumsy, reckless, absent minded and excited. He isn't good at channelling his aggressiveness. This is why he must draw inspiration from Tartuffe's guidelines. Even at the Valenods' house, he allows his emotions to show through and, at the seminary, he is singled out for his inability to be devious. The attempted murder of Madame de Rênal is a good example of the lover's impulsiveness. Even during the trial, he prefers to make a revolutionary rant rather than a careful speech which would have saved him from being beheaded. Julien's ambition cannot hide who he is; he is no Rastignac!

A FAST AND NATURAL PIECE OF WRITING

Stendhal writes quickly with the words that come to him. In a letter written to his sister, Pauline, he explains that the speed at which he writes ensures the text is simple, fluid and clear. This style of writing affects both the content and the structure of his novel:

- It makes the content seem plausible. Stendhal saw *The Red and the Black* as a chronicle in which the events happen one after another without a break. He does not plan the details of each chapter in advance and oversights are corrected along the way. For example, to explain Julien's sudden familiarity with the marquis, the author later explains 'the reader may well be startled by this free and almost friendly tone, but we've forgotten to mention that, for six weeks, the Marquis had been confined to his home by an attack of gout' (Part 2, Chapter 7). Bedridden, Marquis de le Mole had nothing better to do than make conversation with his secretary. Paradoxically, this approach gives the narrator a natural style; we do not notice the underlying planning that is almost too well arranged, unlike with Balzac, Zola or Proust;

- If affects the description of the scenery: long scenes are rare in this story. Of course, Stendhal is aware that it is necessary to depict the material reality of the time period but *The Red and the Black* is not a historical novel; the reader is contemporary to the events. This allows Stendhal to focus on the action;

- The description of the characters is also different as the narrator doesn't introduce them immediately, unlike the three writers mentioned above who describe all of the characters' characteristics before they come into a scene. Stendhal, who seeks to find a natural rhythm, can't afford to interrupt the action to name and describe the characters;

- The syntax is also affected:
  ◦ Punctuation: Stendhal rarely interrupts the flow of a sentence. The comma easily replaces all other punctuation; semi-colons, brackets and even full stops. He also removes speech marks for thoughts and dialogue (without using dashes). However, the colon is used to help us to fully experience each scene. 'All he could see in Madame de Rênal was a rich woman: he let her hand fall, disdainfully, and walked away' (Part 1, Chapter 9).
  ◦ Connectives: along the same lines, few connectives are used in the text. The causality that links the two sentences can be understood without them. Therefore,

there is no need to resort to traditional words like 'therefore', 'in fact' or even 'that is why'.

- ◦ Verb forms: the author prefers verbs in the active form. He removes any present participles and anything that interrupts the word flow.
- Finally, this writing style causes some carelessness which Stendhal himself regrets later. Writing quickly is good; writing too quickly is risky. In his haste, the author effectively botches up some passages.
  - ◦ He uses some clichés, although he hates rhetoric: 'that smile proved fatally illuminating' (Part 1, Chapter 1), 'dissolving into tears' (Part 1, Chapter 9), 'blinded by anger' (Part 1, Chapter 21), 'cruel necessity, with its iron hand, forced Julien to bend his will' (Part 1, Chapter 23), 'his legs were giving way underneath him' (Part 1, Chapter 25), 'a black sheep' (Part 1, Chapter 27), etc.
  - ◦ We can also find some repetition due to inattention. For example, the same Shakespearian extract is used as the epigraph for two chapters. It also says that 'Julien felt himself humiliated', then that he endured 'humiliating silence' (Part 1, Chapter 7). Furthermore, in one paragraph it reads 'his eyes looked but did not see' and then 'he was looking without seeing' (Part 1, Chapter 28). However, these mistakes don't spoil the natural, sincere and familiar style of writing.

FURTHER REFLECTION

SOME QUESTIONS TO THINK ABOUT...

- The novel is divided into two parts. How are they different and what links them together?
- When does Julien use a ladder? Compare these episodes.
- In chapter 19 of the second part, Stendhal uses an ellipsis rather than explaining what happened: in your opinion, why does he do this?
- *The Red and the Black* makes few specific historic references. Why do you think this is?
- Stendhal puts certain words in italics or in inverted commas on multiple occasions. Why is this? Support your idea with examples from the text.
- Through the theme of the plot and Julien's solemn statement in court, which historic events is Stendhal alluding to?
- If you were a juror, would you have condemned Julien Sorel to death? Explain your stance.
- What similarities are there between *The Red and the Black* and *The Charterhouse of Parma*, Stendhal's other great novel (plot, perception of women, characterisation of the hero, etc.)?
- What similarities can be found between *The Red and the Black* and *Madame Bovary* by Flaubert? Furthermore, in what way does Stendhal's novel differ from *La Princesse de Clèves* by Madame de la Fayette and *The New Heloise* by Rousseau?

We want to hear from you!
Leave a comment on your online library
and share your favourite books on social media!

FURTHER READING

REFERENCE EDITION

- Stendhal (2004) *The Red and the Black*. Trans. Raffel, B. New York: Modern Library Classics.

REFERENCE STUDIES

- Beaumarchais, J.-P. and Couty, D., eds. (2001) *Dictionnaire des grandes œuvres de la littérature française*. Paris: Larousse-VUEF.
- Dantzig, C. (2005) *Dictionnaire égoïste de la littérature française*. Paris: Grasset.
- Claudon, F. (1998) Stendhal. in J.-C. Polet, ed., *Patrimoine littéraire européen. 10. Gestation du romantisme*. Brussels: De Boeck Université.
- Klein, C. and Lidsky, P. (1971) *Le Rouge et le Noir. Stendhal*. Paris: Hatier.

www.brightsummaries.com

Ebook EAN: 9782806279569

Paperback EAN: 9782806283412

Legal Deposit: D/2016/12603/317

Cover: © Primento

Digital conception by Primento, the digital partner of publishers.